Chance:
The Incredible,
Wonderful,
Three-Legged Dog
And
Making Friends

A friend loves at all times.....

Proverbs 17:17 (NIV)

To Joe "Hoppy" Sullivan who has spent a lifetime being a good man and a good friend.

Everyone needs a friend.

A friend accepts you just the way you are, even when you are not perfect.

Bernese

Friends come in all shapes and sizes. Friends are big like Harley.

Teacup
Chihuahua

Friends are small like Mugsy.

You may have a friend who is exactly like you...

or not like you at all.

You can learn many things from your friends, and get along with them happily!

Friends take care of you...

and you take care of them.

Friends play with you...

and share with you.

A friend will love you when you are scared or sad...

or
happy!

Be kind to everyone, because everyone needs a friend. You never know who your next friend will be!

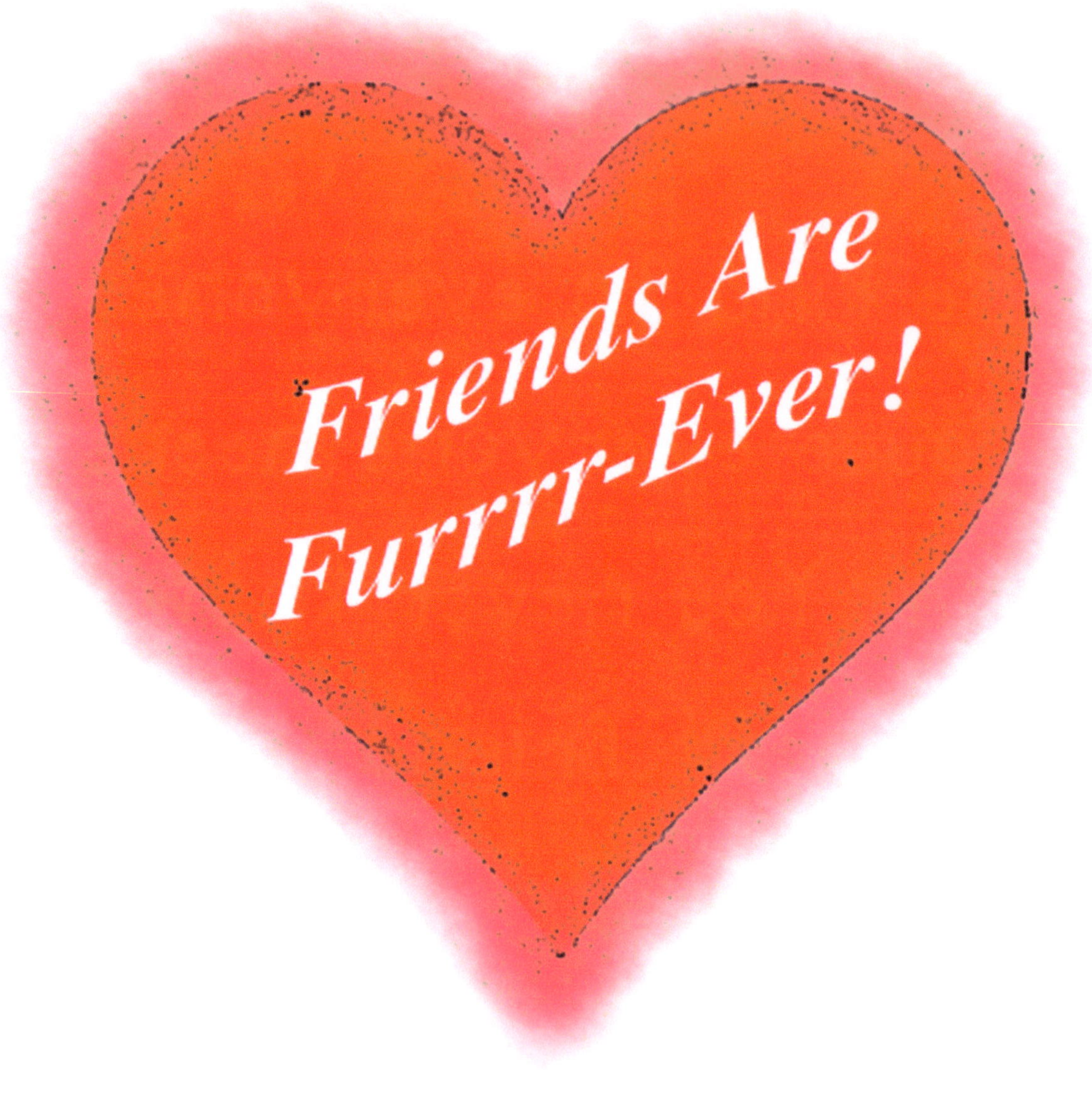
Friends Are
Furrrr-Ever!

The End

Stay tuned for Chance's next adventure!

Complete Dolch Word List Divided by Level

Pre-primer		Primer			Grade One		Grade Two			Grade Three	
a	look	all	he	so	after	let	always	found	their	about	kind
and	make	am	into	soon	again	live	around	gave	these	better	laugh
away	me	are	like	that	an	may	because	goes	those	bring	light
big	my	at	must	there	any	of	been	green	upon	carry	long
blue	not	ate	new	they	ask	old	before	its	us	clean	much
can	one	be	no	this	as	once	best	made	use	cut	myself
come	play	black	now	too	by	open	both	many	very	done	never
down	red	brown	on	under	could	over	buy	off	wash	draw	only
find	run	but	our	want	every	put	call	or	which	drink	own
for	said	came	out	was	fly	round	cold	pull	why	eight	pick
funny	see	did	please	well	from	some	does	read	wish	fall	seven
go	the	do	pretty	went	give	stop	don't	right	work	far	shall*
help	three	eat	ran	what	going	take	fast	sing	would	full	show
here	to	four	ride	white	had	thank	first	sit	write	got	six
I	two	get	saw	who	has	them	five	sleep	your	grow	small
in	up	good	say	will	her	then		tell		hold	start
is	we	have	she	with	him	think				hot	ten
it	where			yes	his	walk				hurt	today
jump	yellow				how	were				if	together
little	you				just	when				keep	try
					know						warm

* 'shall' has dropped out of use

Chance: The Incredible, Wonderful, Three-Legged Dog and Making Friends

Copyright ©2016 Carolyn Sullivan Moore

ISBN 978-1506-911-81-6 PRINT
ISBN 978-1506-902-95-1 EBOOK

LCCN 2015956276

September 2016

Published and Distributed by
First Edition Design Publishing, Inc.
P.O. Box 20217, Sarasota, FL 34276-3217
www.firsteditiondesignpublishing.com

www.ingramcontent.com/pod-product-compliance
Lightning Source LLC
LaVergne TN
LVHW072109070426

835509LV00002B/84